MW00477911

This publication is provided by:
Freedom in Jesus Ministries

A Non-Profit 501 (c) 3 Corporation

www.fijm.org
info@fijm.org

JAIL-HOUSE RELIGION
From Park Avenue... to Park Bench... to Prison

An Inmate's True Experience
Stephen E. Canup
Extended Version

Special thanks to:
Rev. Don Castleberry
Board Chairman and Founder
Freedom in Jesus Ministries

ACKNOWLEDGEMENTS

Everyone needs a mature spiritual mentor and trusted accountability partner. I love and appreciate Don Castleberry for fulfilling this role for me. His trust, time and commitment to me have been invaluable. He and his wife, Donna, have become some of my very best friends.

Rev. Don Castleberry is Founder and Board Chairman, Freedom in Jesus Prison Ministries. Learn more about this anointed prison ministry at www.fijm.org; or, write to Don in care of Freedom in Jesus Ministries, P.O. Box 939, Levelland, TX 79336, or email us at info@fijm.org.

Special thanks to Kevin Rhoads, Dream Taxi Media + Marketing, for the title of Stephen's personal testimony, which also became the sub-title of this book. For more creative and marketing assistance contact Kevin Rhoads: kevin@creativeguy.com

Additional thanks to Rico Vega, Grant Willingham and Taylor Sutherland, Slate Group, for assistance in creative design and lay-out. Also, special appreciation goes to Angella Jordan, Account Representative, Slate Group, Lubbock, TX. For more information on Slate Group services, contact Angella Jordan: angella@slategroup.com

Appreciation is also expressed for additional printing services at Perfection Press. For information contact Robert Riggs, rriggs@printedtoperfection.com

TABLE OF CONTENTS

INTRODUCTION

"Jail-House Religion" – We've all heard that term – usually negatively.

In "the free world" believers and unbelievers alike generally assume an "inmate" who professes to follow Jesus Christ does so to try to bargain with God for an early release; or, to convince their family and the parole board they've changed when perhaps they have really not. Sometimes "free world citizens" are correct in making these assumptions.

Behind the razor wire, steel bars and concrete walls of jails and prisons, Christian inmates are often objects of sarcasm and ridicule by other inmates, and even some of the correctional officers.

Incarcerated Christians regularly hear, in mocking catcalls and jeers, taunts like this:

- "Hey man, you weren't reading your Bible on the street, how come you're reading it now in here?"
- "Hey preacher, I never saw you going to church in the free world, why are you going to all those Chapel services and classes in here?"
- "Choir boy, if you're really a Christian, how come you're locked up? Where's your God now?"

When I was incarcerated, I often heard all those questions, taunts and criticisms about others before I surrendered my life to Jesus Christ (and even more frequently when they were directed at me after I was truly saved). Before I ever went to prison I thought all those jail-house conversions I'd heard about were fake. Surely, "Jail-House Religion" was just a cheap imitation of the real thing.

I was wrong – dead wrong. "Jail-House Religion" can be "the real thing". I know. Jesus found me in prison – broken, battered, bound, betrayed and busted. But He saved me, and changed me forever.

This is my story...

THE "OLD MAN"
Six Months before Prison (2007)
Stephen Canup

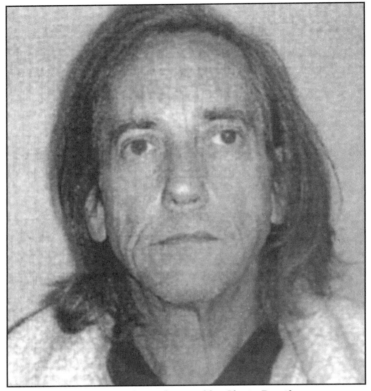

Guilty and Condemned by Sin to Death
Romans 6:23 "For the wages of sin is death...

Guilty of these sins against God, others and self:

Addictions to drugs, alcohol, sex, pornography, praise of men, work

Pride	Judgment	Thievery
Worry	Self-hate	Adultery
Fear	Resentment	Sexual identity
Depression	Regret	Confusion
Hopelessness	Anger	Lying
Anxiety	Covetousness	Conceit
Profanity	Depravity	Intellectualism
Fornication	Reprobation	Humanism
Lustful desires	Un-forgiveness	Shame
Perversion	Immorality	Remorse
Idolatry	Self-abuse	Guilt
Selfishness	Bitterness	Offense

The sinful and cursed life I was living before prison resulted in me being:

- Homeless, living on the streets of Nashville, TN, for 3 years prior to prison.
- Unemployed for 7 years prior to incarceration.
- Broke after having filed for bankruptcy twice.
- Destitute with all my earthly possessions contained in 1 hanging garment bag in the prison's property room awaiting the day of my release.
- Desolate having abandoned all family and friends, leaving me lonely and utterly forsaken.
- Depressed so deeply by these life conditions that I had attempted suicide several times.
- Hopeless and absolutely convinced nothing would ever change or get better in any way.

THE "NEW MAN"
One Year after Prison (2012)
Stephen Canup

A Free Man - Alive in Christ
...but the gift of God is eternal life in Christ Jesus our Lord." Romans 6:23

"I have been crucified with Christ and I no longer live, but Christ lives in me. The life I now live in the body, I live by faith in the Son of God, who loved me and gave himself for me." (Gal. 2:20)

"Therefore if any is (ingrafted) in Christ, the Messiah, he is (a new creature altogether), a new creation; the old (previous moral and spiritual condition) has passed away. Behold, the fresh and new has come!"
(II Cor. 5:17, AMP)

"So if the Son sets you free, you will be free indeed" (John 8:36)

4

The new life in Christ that began in prison in 2009 has brought many blessings. As of early 2017, some of these abundant life realities include:

- My spiritual re-birth April 20, 2009!!!
- Restored relationships with every family member.
- A mentor and accountability partner, Don Castleberry, who speaks the truth in love.
- Acceptance instead of rejection.
- Joy and hope instead of depression and hopelessness.
- Purpose and passion to help set others free.
- Peace, boldness and confidence instead of anxiety and fear.
- The righteousness of Christ Jesus instead of perversion and depravity.
- Love and compassion for others instead of selfishness and self-hate.
- Freedom from addictions to alcohol, drugs, pornography, smoking and gambling.
- A tongue of blessings and respect instead of pride, criticism and profanity.
- A tender, new heart rather than the old heart of stone.
- Re-made to be a cheerful giver of tithes and offerings.
- A beautiful, three bedroom, two bath home provided rent-free except for utilities.
- Two late-model vehicles were given to me in great condition with low mileage.
- A house full of good furniture, and a closet full of good clothes.
- Debt-free, with also some money in savings.
- A renewed mind free of all the bad effects of addictions and depression.
- Good health.
- Mature Christians I can call for prayer or advice anytime about anything.
- Licensed and ordained in 2012 as a minister of the Gospel of Jesus Christ.

JAIL-HOUSE RELIGION
"The Real Thing" or "A Cheap Imitation"?
Stephen E. Canup, 2010, while incarcerated

"Jail-House Religion".... How many times have we heard that phrase? It's usually in a mocking way. Is it "the real thing" or "a cheap imitation"?

Can someone really find God in a jail or prison? Is God close enough to us here to hear our sincere cry? Can we really be heard by Him as we commit, or re-dedicate, our hearts to walk with Christ? What does God say about people like us in His Word? Can He actually use a convict, who turns his life around, to advance the cause of His Kingdom?

We know what "society" says and thinks about us – they call us misfits, outcasts and career criminals. For the most part, they despise us. They think that we are worthless, dangerous and not capable of changing our ways. They are ashamed of us, afraid of us and would like to forget us. When they lock us up we are "out of sight, out of mind". We are at the very bottom of the social ladder – like the bottom of a dark empty well with no ladder to climb out. How low can we go and still find God?

When we are as low as we can go, and think that the only "light at the end of the tunnel" is a train headed our way, what do we do? When we finally wake up one day and realize we are sick and tired of being locked up again and again because of our own stupid actions, wrong decisions, and addictions, who do we turn to?

Isn't this the time and place that makes the most sense to cry out to God?

Think about the story of "The Prodigal Son" – he was eating, sleeping and working among the pigs in the muck and mud. The Bible says in **Luke 15:17**, that he finally "came to his senses", saw the error of his ways, desired forgiveness, and turned back to go home to his father. Sometimes, God uses the worst of conditions at the bottom of our own miry pit to get our attention. **Psalm 118:5** says, "In my anguish I cried to the Lord, and He answered me by setting me free."

In Luke 19:10, Jesus said He "...came to seek and to save what was lost." The religious leaders of the day wanted to know why He ate with and ministered to "sinners". Where are plenty of us lost sinners? Locked up in prison. Jesus is seeking to save us!

In here we are sober and in our right minds. We are "still". If we listen, we can hear Him here!

Seek the Lord

God tells us if we seek Him (look hard for Him), we will find Him! It does not matter where we are, how old we are, what our problems are – if we seek Him, He will be found by us.

> Is. 55:6-7 - "Seek the Lord while He may be found: Call on Him while He is near. Let the wicked forsake his way and the evil man his thoughts. Let him turn to the Lord, and he will have mercy on him, and to our God, for He will freely pardon."

> Jer. 29:11-14 - "For I know the plans I have for you, declares the Lord, plans to prosper you and not to harm you, plans to give you hope and a future. Then you will call upon me and come and pray to me and I will listen to you. You will seek me and find me when you seek me with all your heart. I will be found by you, declares the Lord, and will bring you back from captivity..."

In other words, when we seek God with all of our heart we will find Him – even when we are locked up.

We are in Good Company

Throughout the entire Bible, time after time, we find God using some of the most unlikely people to accomplish His will to advance His Kingdom. He has used murderers, adulterers, thieves, lowly shepherds, hated tax collectors; and, a lot of them had, at one time or another, been in some form of confinement or captivity.

But these men repented, committed their lives to God, and cried out to Him from their own miserable circumstances. People like Peter,

Paul, Samson, James, John the Baptist, Joseph, and Jeremiah had been incarcerated just like us. Leaders like Moses, David, and Jacob – who were once murderers, adulterers and thieves - were used mightily once they called on God and turned their lives back to Him. Even Jesus was arrested and put on trial.

God does not care about your record. Unlike men, God does not discriminate against the down-trodden, the lowly, the forgotten – we who are labeled as felons, prisoners, convicts and inmates.

God has a Special Love for People like Us

God must have a special love and attention reserved for people like us – prisoners, convicts, inmates, and captives. In fact, Strong's Concordance listed over 340 verses where the word "prison", "prisoner", "captive" or captivity" is a key word.

For Example:

Ps. 102:19-20 – "The Lord looked down...from Heaven...to hear the groans of the prisoners..."

Ps. 69:33 – "The Lord... does not despise His captive people..."

Ps. 146:7 – "The Lord sets prisoners free."

Zech. 9:11-12 – "I will free your prisoners from the waterless pit...O prisoners of hope; even now I announce that I will restore twice as much to you."

Matt. 25:36 – Jesus said, "...I was in prison and you came and visited me."

And in one of His first talks in the synagogue, after Satan tempted Him in the wilderness, Jesus quoted:

Is. 61:1 "...the Lord has anointed me to preach good news to the poor. He has sent me to bind up the broken-hearted, to proclaim freedom for the captives and release from darkness for the prisoners..."

Jeremiah, one of the most important and Holy prophets in the Old Testament, was himself falsely accused and was held as a prisoner at the bottom of an old cistern – a hole like a well - dark, damp and deep in the ground.

Jer. 38:6 – "So they took Jeremiah and put him into the cistern... they lowered Jeremiah by ropes into the cistern; it had no water in it, only mud, and Jeremiah sank down into the mud."

But God did not leave him there! Later on, in Jer. 38:11-13, God used a Babylonian ruler, an enemy, to appeal to the King on Jeremiah's behalf. He got permission to pull Jeremiah up out of the pit, not long before he would have starved to death.

God has plenty of experience pulling people up

Just like he did for Jeremiah, God has plenty of experience pulling people up out of their own miry, dark, damp, deep pit. David, a man after God's own heart, must have known exactly what it was like. See if you can see yourself in David's own "pit experience":

Ps. 69:1-3, 5, 14-17 – "Save me, O God, for the waters have come up to my neck. I sink in the miry depths, where there is no foothold. I have come into the deep waters; the floods engulf me. I am worn out calling for help; my throat is parched. My eyes fail, looking for my God... You know my folly, O God; my guilt is not hidden from you... Rescue me from the mire, do not let me sink; deliver me from those who hate me, from the deep waters. Do not let the floodwaters engulf me or the depths swallow me up or the pit close its mouth over me. Answer me, O Lord, out of the goodness of your love; in your great mercy turn to me. Do not hide your face from your servant; answer me quickly, for I am in trouble".

Ps. 40:1-4a – "I waited patiently for the Lord; He turned to me and heard my cry. He lifted me out of the slimy pit, out of the mud and mire; He set my feet on a rock and gave me a firm place to stand. He put a new song in my mouth, a hymn of praise to our God. Many will see and fear and put their trust in the Lord. Blessed is the man who makes the Lord His trust..."

Not only will God rescue you, and pull you up out of your own pit, but He can use your example, your story, and your testimony to bring others to Him!

"You Weren't Reading Your Bible on the Street"

Most people don't know what these scriptures say about how important prisoners are to God and His work, and how much He loves them. So, many inmates taunt Christians with stuff like, "You weren't reading your Bible on the street"; or, "You weren't going to church or chapel services before they locked you up"; or, "Man, that's just that old jail-house religion, it will wear off pretty soon. It's not real. It's just the same old fake stuff we've seen before."

In some ways they're right. I don't know about you, but if I had been caught up in God's Word instead of my addictions, I probably wouldn't have ended up here. If I had been going to church every week instead of going out to beg, borrow or steal enough to get my next hit, I probably wouldn't have ended up here. I'm sick and tired of places like this. I want to be a better man for my family. I need Jesus. I need to change. I want to change.

Do You Have "the Real Thing"?

"Jail-House Religion" can either be "the real thing" or "a cheap imitation". All of us have seen imitation, "knock-off" products – fake Nike tennis shoes, imitation Air-Jordan's, fake designer handbags like Gucci, etc. You can tell the fakes over time, maybe not so much at first, but over time the imitation breaks down, falls apart and gets thrown away. We don't use it anymore. It becomes clear why it was so cheap to begin with.

Unlike when we might have been tricked into buying a fake "knock-off", in our new relationship with God, we determine, through our own actions, habits and beliefs, whether we get "the real thing" or "a cheap imitation". How will we, and others, be able to tell whether our own personal experiences with "Jail-House Religion" result in "the real thing" or just "a cheap imitation"?

Let's compare some of the characteristics of each one:

"The Real Thing" VS	"A Cheap Imitation"
• We try to be serious about it and consistently try to do the right thing.	• We are "on again, off again", inconsistent, like we are "playing with God".
• We allocate regular, significant time daily to God's Word.	• We are too tired or too busy to try to read even the one page devotional from "Our Daily Bread".
• People notice good, positive changes in the way we talk and act.	• By the way we talk or act, our friends might never know or even guess that we are following Christ.
• We have real joy, peace and more genuine love.	• We still hold on to anger, depression and hate.
• When we are released, our Bibles and God go with us.	• When we are released we leave our Bibles behind on our bunks or one of the tables. We leave God behind too.
• After release, we find a good pastor, join the church and attend faithfully.	• After release, we keep "intending" to go to church but we never get around to it.
• We will have fellowship daily with other Christians, and find a Bible study group to challenge us.	• We go right back to our old friends and hang out in the same places.

Choose the Real Thing

Personally, I want "the real thing". God got my attention. I want the rest of my life to be the opposite of my recent past. I don't want to keep coming back here.

They say insanity is doing the same old thing over and over and over again and expecting different results. I might be crazy, but I am not yet insane! When I finally "came to my senses" after my first ten months of incarceration, like "The Prodigal Son", I wanted to go back to my Heavenly Father. I decided I was going to do something different, so I could be different, so I could finally make a difference in my own life, the lives of my family, and in my community.

When it comes to "Jail-House Religion", I want "The Real Thing" – a personal relationship with Jesus Christ as my Savior and Lord! Each of us gets to make our own decision. Have you made this decision? Have you decided to go "all in and all out" for Jesus?

Be encouraged, be strong, be blessed – choose "The Real Thing"! There is no better time to cry out for God. He will hear you. His Word says you are special to Him. He will help you. He loves you wherever, and however, and whoever you are now. You do not have to "change" before you find Jesus. He will change you if you let Him. Just go to Him. He will take care of the rest.

FROM PARK AVENUE...
TO PARK BENCH...TO PRISON
A Personal Testimony of God's Grace and Mercy
Stephen E. Canup

I never dreamed my life testimony would include a period of nearly three years in prison starting at age 56. Yet, I really should not be surprised since I had been running from God, and living against Him, for 20 years. In fact, I had not truly served Him for 40 years. When asked, I told others I was "a Christian", but who did I think I was kidding? I only deceived myself, not God, and I reaped what I sowed (Gal. 6:7-8).

I can only blame myself. I alone accept full responsibility for my actions. I definitely do not blame God. He didn't cause this. He didn't leave me or forsake me – I was the one who left Him. Neither can I blame my "environment" or my family. I was raised in a middle-class home in a good neighborhood by both parents who were dedicated Christians. I cannot blame the justice system. As a first-time offender, I would never have even been locked up for nearly three years if I had only initially obeyed the terms of my probation.

It was my own fault. I gave myself over to worldly temptations, pursuits and pleasures. My addictions to drugs, alcohol, sex and pornography only made matters much worse. Where did I first "go wrong"?

On Top of the World

Twenty years earlier, I was living "the American Dream". I had what, in the world's eyes, was a marvelously successful life. In 1987, at age 35, I was at the top of my profession as a CPA earning a salary well into the six-figures. I had an office on the 27th floor of a high-rise office building on Park Avenue in New York City. I was a partner with the world's largest accounting firm. I had been blessed with a wonderful, Godly wife and a healthy infant son. I would soon have a new, custom built home. The vehicles we drove had no loans against them. My credit record was spotless. I had credit cards with over $100,000 available credit and, except for the mortgage I would have on our new home, I was totally free of consumer debt. By any worldly standard, I was "on top of the world".

Outwardly, I was the definition of success. Inwardly, however, I was lost, confused, bored, empty and restless (Eccl 2:10-11). I was addicted to pride, success, and money. I lived my life to garner the acceptance and good opinions of others. I realize now I had everything but the one thing that mattered - I did not have Jesus. I was not thankful. I did not desire or seek God. I thought I was wise, but I was a fool (Rom. 1:21-22). My conceit, impatience, greed, selfishness and pride were about to destroy my life (Prov. 16:18).

The Long Downward Spiral

In 1989, I suddenly, foolishly and selfishly left my wife and son to pursue worldly desires, fame and riches in Nashville's music business. I became my own "god", determined to create and control my own life. For this vanity and foolish pride, God gave me over to my own desires, lusts and addictions. It was a gradual, but steady, descent over 20 years into sinfulness, depravity and reprobation (Rom 1:24-32).

It didn't take too long to see that I had made a fatal error. Trying to "break in" to the music publishing and writing business was near impossible. The odds of success for me were about the same as me competing in Hollywood for a part in a movie against established actors like Brad Pitt, Leonardo DiCaprio or, back then, Tom Cruise. How stupid I was. For the first time in my life I had failed – and failed miserably. All the money I had, and all I could borrow, had been invested foolishly. I lost it all.

I experienced addictions to alcohol, marijuana, crack cocaine, gambling, sex and pornography. For many years, I was severely and almost continuously in deep depression and often contemplated suicide. There were several failed suicide attempts. Unashamedly, I participated in almost every form of sexual immorality and perversion. I was a spiritual, mental, emotional and financial wreck. I filed bankruptcy twice. I was diagnosed as having bi-polar disorder.

I was so empty inside for so many years. In spite of everything I tried, nothing filled the void in my soul. I felt unworthy of love and, over time, I had pushed away every friend and family member. I was without hope and without God in my world (Eph. 2:12).

From 2002-2008, I was unemployed and existed only by the kindness of strangers and one friend, who loved me in spite of myself. He allowed me to stay rent-free with him for three years. Eventually I alienated even him. I got an apartment and a menial job for a few months (after I could no longer stay with him), but was soon fired and homeless. It was 2006.

I lived in a tent on an undeveloped wooded hillside in South Nashville for 1½ years. Then I lived for 6 months at the Nashville Rescue Mission – a homeless shelter for men. I was there when I was arrested in May, 2008, for violating the terms of my probation. My six-year probated sentence was revoked and I was sent to CCA-Nashville's medium-security prison to serve my time.

Life looked totally hopeless, and I was convinced nothing would ever get better. To me, my life was over, but a merciful and loving God rescued me in spite of myself. Thank God, He was not finished with me yet. I see now that He had His own plan for my life, but He would not begin to reveal it until I finally realized and admitted what a mess and failure I had made after I made myself "god" of my life. I needed to humble myself and submit to Him. I had to surrender.

Jail-House Religion

As you can safely conclude by now, I definitely was not following Jesus before I went to prison. I didn't find Him in prison. He wasn't lost. I was. He found me.

My first act of submission was to ask for a Bible from the Chaplain – a Gideon New Testament which I read daily for about 15 minutes. I remember how hesitant I was at first to openly read my Bible and go to Chapel services. I had already heard plenty of remarks about other Christians in prison regarding "Jail-House Religion". So, for the first ten months

I only read my Bible privately for a few minutes each night. I did not attend Chapel services. I watched TV, played cards and read a lot of spy novels and westerns. None of this got me out of my deep depression or made any positive change in me. Time passed slowly.

I eventually realized I had finally reached bottom. I could not go any lower. I had lost everything. I felt absolutely hopeless. On top of everything else, my crime was "solicitation of a minor" – a charge I picked up during a stretch of five days without sleep fueled by my addictions to crack cocaine, pornography and alcohol. I did some incredibly stupid things resulting in me now being branded as a "sex offender". I now realize God does not see one sin worse than another, but my hopelessness caused me to see it only in the way it is viewed by society.

After 10 months in prison, I finally "came to my senses" like the Prodigal Son (Luke 15:11-24). When I finally surrendered to God, and cried out in true humility and brokenness, He heard me. He lifted me out of the miry pit of hopelessness and despair. He placed my feet solidly on His Rock - Jesus (Psalm 40:1-3).

On April 20, 2009, my 57th birthday, I re-dedicated my life to Jesus Christ. I was re-baptized while I was in prison too. I confessed my sins, sincerely repented, and asked Jesus to take over my life. What a heavy burden of guilt, shame, remorse and embarrassment I had been carrying. As I finally submitted to Him, these burdens were lifted off my soul and spirit.

Even though I was still locked up, I was "free on the inside"! Jesus became not only my Savior, but I made Him truly my Lord and put Him in charge. I decided I was going to go "all in and all out" for Jesus - a decision I have never once regretted, not even for a minute!

As I began to read the Bible, I became convinced that through Jesus, my future could be totally new and different from my past. When I realized that God could find me and change me even in prison, I wanted to know as much as I could about pursuing a relationship with Him. I ignored snide and sarcastic comments about "Jail-House Religion"; "You weren't going to church before you got here, why are going to Chapel services here, choirboy?"; and, "You weren't reading your Bible on the street, why are you reading it in here?"

I knew God was real because He was changing me gradually, but completely, from the inside out. The changes I felt were not "forced" by me, but were occurring primarily as a result of spending more time deliberately in His Word and prayerfully in His presence.

My boldness and commitment to diligently seek Him increased dramatically as I began to realize how many times the Bible talks about "prisoners" and "captivity". I found out how many men God was able to use who were once murderers, adulterers, liars, thieves and reprobates. Many of them spent time as a prisoner. God has a way of showing His strength in man's weakness (II Cor. 12:9-10)!

I began to ignore all the remarks from unbelievers who did not want to change their lives or circumstances. The more time I spent seeking after God, the more hopeful, joyful and fulfilled I became. I refused parole and decided instead to discharge my sentence. The next twenty-two months seemed to fly by after I decided to treat my remaining months in prison like I was in "Bible College" or "Bible Boot Camp".

I know, in my case, that "Jail-House Religion" was "the real thing", not "a cheap imitation". The changes in me have been permanent, not temporary. In prison, I committed to spending significant, quality time seeking God daily, and I have continued this daily time with God since my release. I have never been disappointed in any way from my diligent pursuit of His wisdom, knowledge, understanding and truth (Heb. 11:6; Pr. 9:10; Psalm 1:1-3; Jn. 14:6). Now, instead of the oppressive emotional and heavy spiritual burdens I had carried for so long, the Holy Spirit within me has filled me with the incredible lightness of His fruit – more love, real joy, true peace, increased patience and self-control, etc. (Gal 5:22-25).

God's Forgiveness

I was saved as a young boy in a Baptist church where my family attended. However, for most of my life I did not attend church or make any serious attempt to follow Jesus. As you now can imagine, there were many things I had done contrary to God. In the poor spiritual and emotional state I lived for so long prior to re-dedicating my life, I believed that I had "gone too far and done too much" for God to forgive me. I was overcome with guilt, regret, remorse and shame. Have you ever felt this way?

I read in a booklet by RBC Ministries, "The Forgiveness of God", that "If we believe our emotions, we may feel we have gone too far. Our self-contempt seems deserved. But there's hope. God wants us to believe in His ability to forgive sins we cannot forget." Our Heavenly Father is angry at sin, but "His anger is not a denial of His love...The truth is that His love is equal to His anger, and because of His love He found a way to show mercy." He sent His Son, Jesus.

It was great news to me when I learned that my sin was forgiven. My guilt was removed. By one Man, once and for all! "Because of the un-limited scope of Christ's death on the cross, we have received forgiveness not only for past sins, but for all sins – past, present, and future... The moment we trust Christ as Savior, we are given immunity from punishment. The issue is settled: Our case is closed and God will not open the files of our guilt again. Just as the courts of earth honor the principle of double jeopardy, heaven will not judge twice those whose sins have been punished in Christ. We will not be tried again for the sins He bore in our place."

Jesus was made sin with our sinfulness, so that we could be made righteous with His righteousness. The Father declares as righteous all those who appeal to the death of Christ as payment for their sin. No sin is excluded. We are saved by grace alone through faith alone in Jesus Christ alone. There is nothing in the entire universe more powerful than the Blood of Jesus that takes away our sin. When we do not deny the Spirit - and thereby accept by faith what Jesus did for us - there is no sin (and no sinner) beyond God's love and forgiveness.

My many sins were taken away! This was a "break-through" realization for me. I knew I could start over. I found present and eternal hope, and freedom in Jesus, when I accepted the Father's forgiveness! Have you finally and fully accepted His mercy, love and forgiveness?

Forgiving Myself

After I truly accepted the Father's forgiveness, He began to show me the importance of forgiving myself, so that my past would stay in the past. That way, I could be unburdened of the guilt, shame, regret, remorse and embarrassment I had been carrying for so long. When I finally put my past behind me, I began to trust God one day at a time with my future (Phil. 3:13-14; Isaiah 43:18-19).

After I had been in prison long enough to be free of all the physical effects of my addictions, I began to think more clearly. I was honest with myself and God. I realized I hated myself for what I had done to ruin my life. I never blamed anyone else – only me – for the poor choices I made, one after another, that eventually led me to prison. I was angry at "me". I hated "me". In fact I could not even look at myself in the mirror as I was shaving or brushing my teeth because I was so disappointed for having foolishly wasted so much of my life, and for mis-using the talents God had given me.

I had broken relationships with, and pushed away, all my friends and family. Having been homeless for most of the three years leading up to my incarceration, I was left with no material possessions other than what was zipped-up inside a single, hanging garment bag in the prison's property room. And now I was a convicted sex offender. I was convinced there was no hope of anything ever getting better. I thought my future could never be any better than my past.

I will never forget the first glimmer of hope I experienced as I began to accept the Father's forgiveness of me and the removal of all my sin – past, present and future. I had never experienced the peace, emotional freedom and mental release I felt when He showed me I must forgive myself, so I could trust Him and move forward as the "new creature"

He made me when I was "born again". I had to make a deliberate and determined choice to "let the past be the past".

It was clear to me that God had forgiven me, but I couldn't forgive myself. Did you ever feel this way?

One day I read something that made me think, "If the blood of Jesus was good enough for God the Father to forgive me, isn't it good enough for me to forgive myself? Who am I to require more than God does for forgiveness of sin? Am I better or more important than God?" Certainly not!

I finally realized there is absolutely nothing I could do about the past. Guilt, shame, regret, remorse and embarrassment had overwhelmed me for far too long. It had paralyzed me with fear, anxiety and depression, all of which kept me from moving forward. I was stuck. I decided that, more than anything else, I needed and wanted to trust God with my future.

I accepted the truth of His Word that He no longer held my past against me. He showed me I too had to stop holding my past against myself. I needed to accept His forgiveness, forgive myself, and move on. Are you stuck? Do you also need to forgive yourself?

Giving and Receiving Forgiveness

In my sin, I had in one way or another offended all my family and friends. I had pushed or driven everyone away. As I began to learn about forgiveness, I sensed that I needed to get past my pride so that I could humble myself to ask forgiveness from the ones I had offended who I could go ahead and contact from inside prison. At first, it was my two older brothers and my younger sister. I felt a burden begin to lift off of me as I wrote and mailed those first letters asking for forgiveness.

It was a great experience to hear my name called at "mail call" for the first time in the ten months that I had then been incarcerated. My two brothers quickly answered me, and let me know they were not holding anything against me. They both expressed their regret for where I was and why I was there, but they also both asked if they could do anything to help me.

God showed me that it might just be possible to receive forgiveness from others if I would just humbly ask.

With my sister, however, it took until after I had been released and walking out my Christian life for a time, before she forgave me. I had offended her the most. But, praise God, our relationship has been restored, and we are closer than we have been in a long time.

My son was the same way. In spite of the many letters I wrote him, he never responded while I was incarcerated. But in early 2013, two years after my release, God arranged a wonderful reunion meeting of reconciliation. What a blessing!

As I continued to study the Word during my incarceration, I also learned that I needed to forgive those who had offended and hurt me throughout my life. That was difficult at first, but I made a conscious decision to forgive them. All the bad feelings, and desire to get even, that I had been carrying was hurting only me. I decided to just give it all up and let it go.

What I discovered was that when we hold un-forgiveness towards someone, it causes a root of bitterness in us – a stronghold for the enemy. Like the unforgiving servant in **Matthew 18:21-35**, we turn ourselves over to "the tormenters" of anger, resentment, hatred, temper, and control – all of which can lead to retaliation, violence and even murder.

A "seed" of un-forgiveness planted in a "ground of hurt" gives us a "harvest" of pain. It grieves our spirit, torments our mind, and distresses us emotionally. All these, combined with a desire for vengeance or retaliation, hurt us - not the person who offended us. Often times they may not even realize their offense. This has been likened to drinking poison ourselves, thinking it will kill the other person! This is madness, and totally self-destructive.

One of the primary reasons Jesus came was so we could have forgiveness through His blood. One of the last things Jesus did was to cry out to God, asking His Father to forgive those who had spit upon Him, ridiculed

Him, beat Him, mocked Him, and nailed Him to that cross. I'm sure he did not "feel" like forgiving them, yet that's what He chose to do, and prayed to His Father in like manner. We must also be willing to love and pray for those who have harmed us. We must be willing to forgive them. Aren't there people you too should choose to forgive?

Freedom from Addictions

Many people in "the free world" are in self-imposed, self-constructed prisons. Whether we are in an actual prison behind razor wire, or not, people everywhere struggle with "addictions" that negatively impact their lives - such as pride, selfishness, depression, anger, pornography, alcohol, prescription medicines, illegal drugs and many others. We may have been enslaved by them for many years. I know I was certainly in a prison of my own making many years before I was actually incarcerated.

Oftentimes, we indulge in addictive behavior to try to fill up the emptiness we feel inside and/or to avoid thinking about and dealing with the root causes of the addictions. At first, dealing with the underlying issues is emotionally painful, and our natural tendency is to avoid pain, even when something good like freedom awaits us on the other side. But the Word of God is clear that Jesus took all our pain, shame, guilt and sin on Himself when He hung on the Cross.

He took all our burdens on Himself so we could be free to live and walk in the abundantly blessed life He planned for us.

Most of us are familiar with the last part of **John 8:31-32**, "you shall know the truth and the truth will set you free". Almost all of us who have been incarcerated have seen it quoted in courtrooms. In actual fact, the truth did not set me free; rather it got me locked up!

I did not realize that the freedom promised as a result from knowing the truth is dependent on the verse preceding it regarding obedience to the teachings of Jesus. If we "hold" to His teaching we are true followers - the pre-condition for "knowing the truth". Who is the Truth? **Jesus (John 14:6)**. So that means that to the extent we know, obey and follow Jesus, the truth of His teachings will set us free! This was truly a new revelation of what had always been a very familiar verse, even to a "heathen" like I once was.

As I studied this sometime after my release, the Spirit prompted me to meditate on how this applied to me. I had determined in 2009 to radically follow Jesus, and do my best to obey His teachings. Certainly I was growing in the knowledge of Him as "the Truth" as I studied His Word and spent quality time in His Presence daily. Consequently, for quite some time, I had in fact realized inside me a freedom I had never experienced before (accompanied by real joy and true peace). But as I thought deeper about this I asked myself, "What has the truth set me free from?"

The Spirit prompted me to make a list of oppressions, strongholds and addictions that I was once in bondage to, but from which I have now been set free. The list you saw earlier on page 3 of this booklet was the result. Believe me, like Paul, I was "the chief of sinners" – it is a very long list - and I add to it as the Spirit reveals. Why have I chosen to be this embarrassingly direct and transparent with you? Because I want you to know that if God can change me so miraculously inside and out, He can change anybody! Do you want to be forever finished with being a slave to old strongholds and addictions?

I am truly free of all those things and I have not been seriously tempted to return to any of them because I quickly take captive every "old man" thought the enemy brings. I know now that those thoughts and temptations the enemy throws at me daily all belong to the "old man" who is now "dead" (Romans 6:6-7). I am a new creature (II Cor. 5:17)! I do not let Satan convince me to resurrect that old, dead man! Therefore, I now experience daily the freedom and liberty of an abundant, over-flowing LIFE in Christ! I know who I am now in Him!

This is only accomplished by totally surrendering daily to the leadership of the Holy Spirit in my life. I am dead, and the life I live now is not me, but Christ living in me, by His Holy Spirit (see Gal. 2:20).

If God can save me and set me free (and He has), He can save anyone and free them from every form of bondage. Yes, this really does include you! Jesus has liberated us to live an abundant life. Don't remain enslaved. Let Jesus set you free and choose to stay free!

The Key to Staying Free

One of the most important things I had to learn in order to remain free from addictions, resist temptations and overcome depression was how to "take my thoughts captive to the obedience of Christ". See **II Corinthians 10:3-5.**

As Joyce Meyers described, the battlefield is in the mind! Sometimes it may seem we fight against impossible odds. The enemy wants you to believe it is always a battle, and it is always uphill. But I want you to know that God has already provided the victory and it is relatively easy to maintain it. Do you want to know the secret?

We often hear people say "resist the devil and he will flee" (**James 4:7b**), but many don't realize that the enemy does not have to flee if you don't first "submit to God" (**James 4:7a**); and then, after resisting the devil and his demons, we must "draw near to God so that God draws near to us" (**James 4:8**).

So the secret I have learned is to "submit to God" first as soon as I discern the enemy's attack when he tries to plant his deceitful lies and thoughts in my mind. By submitting first to God I can successfully recognize and resist the wrong thoughts, and take them captive by rejecting them and filling my mind instead with the thoughts of God.

How does one "submit to God"? By countering the lies, accusations and hopelessness of the enemy with the truth, acceptance and eternal hope of the Word of God. We must know what God says about us in His Word in order for us to successfully combat and take captive what the enemy says about us, or accuses us with. And when we confess God's Word about our situation we are able to "draw near to God". Doesn't this make good sense?

For example, we read in Luke 4:1-14, that Jesus Himself countered the enemy's temptations successfully when He came out of the wilderness by recognizing the devil's voice and responding to him with the Word of God. Note that the Word Jesus utilized was very specific to the area of temptation. Jesus knew what the Word said and used it to counter the enemy. We must do likewise.

(By the way, did you notice that Jesus was full of the Spirit, and led by the Spirit, in the wilderness; and, also was in the power of the Spirit coming out of the wilderness (Luke 4:1 and 4:14)? If Jesus had to have the Holy Spirit, so do we! As I will discuss later, the empowerment of the Holy Spirit is critical for us in every area of our walk in Christ. But I digress...)

So, what is the secret to knowing the truth disclosed in the Word of God regarding His thoughts about us as "new creations in Christ"? I believe the secret is to daily confess aloud what the Word of God says about us, and to pray personalized daily prayers to ask the Father to help us apply the Word to our lives in every situation.

Let me recommend something to you. While I was still incarcerated, two different ministers encouraged me to begin the practice of agreeing daily with God about what His Word says about me, and praying powerful, personalized daily prayers over my life. I typed these up after my release, and I am enclosing them near the end of this book for your review and use.

I encourage you to repeat these daily for six months, even if you only whisper loud enough where only you hear it. "Faith comes by hearing, and hearing by the Word of God" according to Romans 10:17. These daily confessions are so very powerful because they are all directly from the Word of God. And praying the Word of God is the most powerfully effective request of the Father that you could ever possibly pray!

We must know what God says about us so that we can recognize and reject the lies of the enemy, taking captive every thought to the obedience of Christ. I challenge you to confess and pray these daily for an extended period. After six months continue to recite them at least weekly thereafter. I promise you they will change the way you speak, think, pray and act.

Repentance

Clearly, everything that happened in my life leading up to prison was not what God had planned and intended for me. Rather, it was the result of my slow, steady, downward spiral into utter depravity. See **Romans 1:18-32**. If your Bible had pictures in it, mine would be there, for this was certainly a picture of me.

God turned me over to my own perverted and misguided, selfish desires which led to a "reprobate" mind – one that can rationalize and do the most evil, despicable things and still convince itself that they are good and acceptable. I was "dead" – like a walking zombie – in my sin and self-deception.

Like the prodigal son (**Luke 15:11-24**), when I came to my senses in prison 10 months into my stay of 32 months, I was empty. I had a "longing" for something more than what I had available to me in my sin, my mess. I longed to "go home". The parable of the prodigal son really got my attention. I could really identify with him. He demonstrated for me that true repentance is "brokenness", and a change of life-direction.

I learned that repentance is not an emotion – for example, not the feeling of "I am sorry", or, "I feel bad about what I've done" – rather, it is a decision. It is like deciding to make a "U-turn" on a highway. You are then headed in the opposite direction from where you were going. Someone in true repentance does not just say "I'm sorry I did that"; they will also live a different life demonstrating a new mind-set of "I won't do it again".

The Greek words translated as "repentance" in the New Testament mean "to think differently", "to change your mind", "to turn about in opinion", "to turn about from an intended way"; and, Webster's Dictionary defines it as "to turn from sin and resolve to reform one's life".

In order for me to return to the Father, I had to go by way of repentance. True repentance is the only way to salvation in and through Jesus Christ. Has true repentance changed your direction? Have you made a "U-turn"?

Jesus Christ is the Only Way – Do Not Be Deceived!
When four of Jesus' closest disciples went to Him privately to ask Him what would be the signs of His Second Coming and of the "end of the age", Jesus warned them several times not to be deceived. Surely, we are even now seeing all the signs come to pass before our very eyes just as He foretold. Likewise, we are already seeing signs of the great deception.

I believe the greatest part of this deception is to try to convince the world that there are more ways to God and Heaven than just through Jesus. THAT IS A LIE. DO NOT BE DECEIVED. The only way to Father God is through the finished work of Jesus Christ of Nazareth at the cross and through His resurrection.

Many are suggesting that Jesus is just one way to Heaven, not necessarily the only way. This has reportedly come from even a few influential leaders within "Christian" circles! It is heresy to espouse this view.

In this age of secular humanism where mankind says they determine their own fate and future, not God, we as Christians are susceptible to their attempts to convince everyone that truth is "relative" to what is going on in society, and so it changes with the times. We are urged to be tolerant of everyone for every reason. No-one must be "offended". We are told that everyone must be "included" and not "confronted" in any way about anything.

While we must certainly treat those who do not agree with us with respect, kindness and gentleness, we must be very careful not to compromise on Who we know is Truth - the Son of God, Jesus Christ. Jesus makes it very clear that He is the only way, the only truth and the only life. He assures us that no-one gets to the Father except through Him (see John 14:6).

Peter preached about this truth about Jesus in **Acts 4:12** when he said, "Salvation is found in no one else, for there is no other name under heaven given to mankind by which we must be saved." Isaiah quotes Jehovah, Father God, in **Isaiah 43:11** as saying, "I, even I, am the Lord, and apart from me there is no savior."

I urge you to study carefully what Jesus revealed in **Matthew 24, Mark 13,** and **Luke 21**. Paul gives us further insight in **1 Thessalonians 4:13 – 5:11; 2 Thessalonians 2:1-17; 1 Timothy 4:1-2;** and **2 Timothy 3:1-5**. Read the visions of Daniel the prophet in **Daniel chapters 7, 11** and **12**. Of course, John tells us about the end of the age in **Revelation**. After studying these passages, I am certain you will agree that surely these times in which we are living are "the last days".

Brothers and Sisters, there is a sense of urgency in me to implore you to be careful you are not deceived – Jesus Christ of Nazareth is the only way to the Father in Heaven. Ask the Father for keen discernment through His Holy Spirit to recognize and avoid the coming great deception.

Jesus is coming back for His people (**John 14:1-3**).

He is coming quickly, in an instant of time (**Matthew 24:27**).

Jesus is coming soon, any day now (**Revelation 22:12-13**).

Are you sure you're ready (**Matthew 24:42-44**)???

Holy Spirit Empowerment

When I was still incarcerated I saw several Christians who were released before me leave, only to return to prison within a year or so. I had also heard of others who had been following Jesus in prison with me that, after their release, fell away from their relationship with Jesus Christ and returned to "the world". I don't know if they returned to a physical prison, but they returned to their emotional and spiritual prisons from which they had once been set free. I know most of them had every good and honest intention to keep walking with Him, but many were powerless to resist old habits, places, and people.

Since I have been released, however, I know personally many former offenders who were transformed in prison, and who are still walking in Christ many years later. They are strong soldiers in God's army. I have seen God working in the lives of their families. I have seen them continue to prosper and experience the abundant life Jesus came to give us (John 10:10). Many have their own effective ministries now. Broken relationships have been restored. Broken hearts have been healed.

What makes the difference in these two groups of people? What made the difference with me? It was clearly the "baptism in the Holy Spirit". I firmly believe that the extra level of empowerment brought about by being baptized (immersed) in the Holy Spirit makes all the difference in enabling and empowering us to walk out our faith effectively and genuinely in prison and then, after our release, in "the free world".

When we accept the finished work of Jesus at the Cross, and confess His resurrection as the Son of God, the Holy Spirit comes to live in us. We "possess" the Spirit, and He begins His ongoing work of sanctification to steadily make our "new man" conform to the image of Christ. However, true empowerment – God's own power – comes to us, and for us, as we totally submit to the Holy Spirit and allow Him to "possess" us - one giant step more than us merely "possessing" Him inside us. We actually are able to allow Him to "possess" us!

We are baptized (immersed) into water as an outward representation of the inward change in us. We are buried with Christ in baptism (our "old man" died); and, we are raised to walk in newness of life (our "new man" came alive). But the Book of Acts makes it clear we should also desire to be baptized (immersed) into the Holy Spirit to receive the same power that resurrected Jesus from the dead – the power to walk out this new life in the way He desires for us. He in us, and us in Him!

We know the verse that says, "Greater is He that is in me than He that is in the world" (I John 4:4). So, the Holy Spirit is in us. We possess Him. But another verse we know is "I can do all things through Him who strengthens me" (Phil. 4:13). That verse is also translated as, "I can do all things through the One who empowers me within". It is the Holy Spirit that empowers us within so that we can do everything the Father desires for us to do, and assigns us to do! But we must let Him do it. We must let Him possess us.

When Jesus finished His work on earth and returned to the Father, the Father sent the Holy Spirit to earth for each of us. Jesus' followers at that time were instructed to wait until they were endued with power from on High before they began to carry out the ministry of Jesus. We should do likewise, that is, we should seek the power of the Holy Spirit before we move out among the people in the name of Jesus. We need the power of the Holy Spirit. Using only our own strength, we will burn out quickly, we will not be effective, and we can even do harm to His Kingdom.

Above all, we must remember the Holy Spirit is a person, He has a personality, and He can be grieved. His purpose in coming was to teach, lead, guide, correct, protect and comfort – the Helper who would walk alongside us as well as dwell within us. However, we must yield to Him and allow Him to do His work in us. If we refuse Him, resist Him, or grieve Him, we will restrict the work that the Father wants Him to do in our lives. He is a gift from the Father, and we need Him!

Paul depended upon the power of the Holy Spirit for his life and ministry. See, for example, **Romans 15:17-19; II Corinthians 12:9; Ephesians 3:16-21**; and, **Colossians 1:29**. In fact, Paul warned Timothy to stay away from religious people in the last days who deny the power of God, the Holy Spirit (see **II Timothy 3:1-7**).

Jesus needed the power of the Holy Spirit too! See **Matthew 3:16-17; Matthew 4:1; Luke 4:1; Luke 4:14; Luke 4:18-19**; and, **Acts 10:38**.

If Jesus, Paul and the other Apostles needed the Holy Spirit, surely we too must have all of God, the Holy Spirit, that He will give us! HE is the "game-changer" for our walk in the Christian life. I urge you to learn as much as you can about your Helper, Teacher, Counselor, Guide and Friend. Near the back of the book I am including more detailed information and scripture references about the Holy Spirit and His Baptism of fire and power. Would you study these prayerfully and deliberately?

We thank the Father for His gifts. He not only gave us His Son, Jesus, but He gave us His Holy Spirit. What a marvelous Father He is. When I think about it, I realize how gullible we are to believe the enemy's lie — the lie that the Holy Spirit is not for today, that we don't need Him. If anything, the truth is we need Him even more because we are living in the last of the last days when Scripture tells us that many will be deceived. The Holy Spirit can help us to not be deceived if we will let Him lead us, and recognize that we "host" Him as the very Presence of God in us. We need Him. We need Him in His fullness.

Have you asked the Father for Jesus to baptize you with the Holy Spirit (Luke 3:16)? If you ask the Father, He will give Him to you (Luke 11:13). Have you allowed the "rivers of living water" to flow from within you (John 7:38-39)? Our Father desires for us to walk in all His fullness by His Holy Spirit.

Surrender, Submission and Sanctification

Before I was saved in prison I wanted to change my life but was powerless to do so. I learned that I could not change me. If I could've changed me I would have done so long before I was addicted, depressed, suicidal, homeless, lonely, lost, and eventually incarcerated! Is this also true of you? Have you tried to change yourself?

I tried to change myself an endless number of times but failed every time. So it was really great news to me that God did not expect me to change myself! Really. He only wanted me to allow His Holy Spirit to possess me, be willing daily to allow Him to lead me in the right way, and try my best to be instantly obedient to His promptings.

When we willingly surrender to God the Holy Spirit in us, and daily submit to be led by His Spirit instead of being led by our "flesh", He will begin His work of sanctification in us! Think about that. In other words, when we surrender to the Spirit, and submit to His leadership moment by moment, He will change us. We are not responsible for changing ourselves. Isn't that good news?

The best picture of submission is one of clay in a potter's hands. The potter transforms the clay from a shapeless handful of ugly mud into an exquisite object of beautiful art. The potter is totally in charge of the transformation, and the end product is determined in large part by his patience and skill. See **Jeremiah 18:1-6; Isaiah 64:8; Romans 9:20-21**.

As followers of Jesus, we can be sure we have the best Master Potter! The Father has sent us His Holy Spirit to accomplish this in us but we must cooperate fully with Him.

Sometimes God allows extreme circumstances, like prison or other hardships of life, to get our attention. Often these may come as a consequence of poor choices made by ourselves or others, but they are best viewed as opportunities for positive change. To be transformed, a piece of clay must be soft so it will yield. We must consciously and willingly submit to God the Holy Spirit.

Regardless of how bad a mess we have made of our lives, and how far we may have run away from God, we are never so broken or so lost that God cannot find us (**Luke 15:4-7**), joyfully accept our returning to Him (**Luke 15:32**), make us a new creation (**II Corinthians 5:17**) and establish His plan for our lives (**Jeremiah 29:11-14**).

However, we must be gratefully humble, prayerfully submissive and faithfully obedient. In humility we must recognize we cannot re-make ourselves and be grateful He can. In submission we must prayerfully put ourselves in His hands and patiently allow Him to form us, and subject us to the hardening fire of trials and circumstances. We must be always faithful in obedience to follow His instructions so that we will experience the best of His intentions as He accomplishes His will through us, forming us into the image of His Son (**Romans 8:29**).

The Word tells us that "His Divine Power has given us everything we need for life and godliness" (**II Peter 1:3**) and that He "teaches us to say 'No' to ungodliness and worldly passions, and to live self-controlled, upright and godly lives in this present age" (**Titus 2:12**). We must receive everything He has given us and be willing to say "No" to worldly temptations. He will help us if we let Him.

It is the sanctifying work of the Spirit that allows us to be obedient to Jesus Christ (**1 Peter 1:2**). As obedient children we are encouraged and empowered by His Holy Spirit not to "conform to the evil desires we once had when we lived in ignorance. But just as He who called you is holy, so be holy in all you do." (**1 Peter 1:14-15**). In our own strength this is impossible, but all things are possible with God the Holy Spirit doing the work of sanctification in us.

Near the back of this book I have included two prayers for submission I think you will find helpful. Pray them to the Father as you are led by His Holy Spirit. It is His job to change you. Your job is to willingly surrender, submit and be obedient to what He wants to do in His ongoing process of sanctification in you.

Transformation

I am so thankful God impressed upon me to use those last 20 months of confinement as a time to grow spiritually in His Word and, thereby, to be "transformed by the renewing" of my mind (**Rom. 12:1-2**). I quit letting my "time do me" and started "doing my time". I quit watching TV and playing cards. Instead, the Spirit motivated me to spend that time in spiritual education and Christian life training programs sponsored by the Chaplain. Additionally, many Bible correspondence courses, frequent Chapel service attendance and intense personal Bible Study hours prepared a solid foundation for me and sowed seed in fertile ground.

I am now a living witness of the Father's grace, mercy, forgiveness and power in Christ Jesus. The Holy Spirit has never been more real to me. The differences in me are real and permanent. God has changed me from the inside out. My attitudes, thoughts, desires and speech have all drastically changed. I am truly a "new creature in Christ – old things are passed away, everything has been made new" (II Cor. 5:17).

After having now experienced the fullness, love, joy and peace of God in Christ Jesus, it is absolutely unthinkable that I would ever again be lured by Satan back into the emptiness, self-hate, anxiety and depression of that "old man" and his addictions. Truly, the Father's love and abiding presence of His Holy Spirit have worked a life-saving miracle in me through Jesus Christ! You can be certain He can do the same for you.

Do Your Time Wisely

I am often asked what kinds of things I did in prison after I got saved but before I went home. As I stated earlier, I planned out every day as to how I could pursue more of God during my waking hours. I tried to separate myself as best I could from all the worldly activities going on around me such as watching TV, reading newspapers, playing cards, and the usual kinds of conversations most inmates have in prison. I'm certain you know what I'm talking about.

There was a verse I remember that really got my attention and I tried to apply it to my situation: "Be very careful, then, how you live - - not as unwise but as wise, making the most of every opportunity, because the days are evil. Therefore, do not be foolish, but understand what the Lord's will is." (Ephesians 5:15-17). We all know how much evil there is around us, especially in prison. God's will is for us to separate ourselves from it, and use our time wisely in living for Him.

I tried to focus as much as possible on studying the Word, memorizing scripture verses, and attending every sort of Chaplaincy class and almost every Christian worship service available to me. I completed many Correspondence Bible Study courses, and for one of them I earned a Study Bible for satisfactorily completing the course. What a wealth of information it contained in its verse commentaries, articles, concordance, subject index and maps!

While you are still incarcerated, for however brief or lengthy a time that may be, make a decision now to use your time wisely. Further your education. Study the Word and learn how to apply it to your daily life. Seek the Father diligently with all your heart. Cultivate an intimate, personal relationship with the Father through His Holy Spirit living in you. Choose to be led by the Spirit moment by moment, instead of being constantly influenced by fleshly desires, the world, or the devil and his demonic hosts.

The Holy Spirit is your teacher. He will help you. Pray often for wisdom, knowledge, understanding, truth, revelation, discernment, and how to apply them to your life. These are all things God wants you to have so He will give them if you ask. He has a plan and a hope-filled future for you.

God wants to use you right where you are. Many people tell me they want to "do prison ministry" when they are released. But I tell them that the most important person in prison ministry is the turned-on, committed Christian still locked up. That is the person who can see firsthand who needs help, who needs prayer, who needs encouragement – right there on the inside. In fact, I believe if you are not already engaging in prison ministry on the inside, you won't do it effectively, if at all, on the outside.

You should become a prayer warrior by praying boldly and diligently for the lost souls around you, for the officers in your unit, for the facility's administration, and for your family. In fact, praying for your family is one of the most powerful and beneficial gifts you can give them. As I learned to pray inside prison I saw the Lord move in mighty ways that built my faith and made me want to pray more!

If your unit offers a faith-based housing area, apply for it. Attend every sort of Chaplaincy program and service that is offered. Read as many Christian books as possible. If your facility offers a spiritual mentorship program, apply for that too. Volunteer for your Chaplain. Get involved with the inside church.

Don't expect perfection from anyone in the church. Just do the best you can to walk your talk (1 Peter 2:11-12). As you know, people are watching, and wanting to know if your commitment is real. In fact, many privately hope it is real because it would mean more hope for them that they too could be changed by a real encounter with our living Lord Jesus.

If you mess up, get up, confess your sin to the Father (I John 1:9), and keep headed in the right direction. Pay no attention to snide remarks from others. At judgment day, you will be standing in front of the King alone. Focus on pleasing Him daily instead of pleasing others. Make wise use of your time. You will be glad you did!

Going Home

As you look forward to the day you will be released, if you are like me you may wonder if you can really follow Christ out there "in the free world". You can. But it will require daily focus and commitment.

If I were to name nine most important things to help you be consistent and faithful about your commitment to follow Christ in "the free world", they would be:

1. Join a church and attend as often as possible.
2. Restore broken relationships - and work at maintaining them once restored.
3. Separate totally and permanently from the former bad influences of certain people, places and things.
4. Faithfully maintain prayer, Bible study and private worship daily.
5. Maintain a constant, prayerful attitude of gratefulness and humility towards God.
6. Get an accountability partner and meet regularly. Having a trusted accountability partner is an important factor in maintaining a faithful walk. It is very hard to try to do it alone.
7. Get actively involved in serving in an anointed ministry as a volunteer. As you invest yourself in the issues and challenges of others, the joy of the Lord will strengthen and enrich you. You will be drawn closer to the Father by the Holy Spirit, and your personal testimony will encourage others.
8. If you fall, quickly confess and truly repent. Get right back up on your Christian walk.

9. Forgive yourself. You did your time – put the past behind you and move on! You are a new creation (II Cor. 5:17)!!

His Call on My Life

God has called me to minister to His lost and forgotten children – inmates, ex-cons, homeless, bi-polar, those who are depressed, addicts and sex offenders. Since I am now, or have recently been, "classified" as each one of these, the Father is using my experiences to reach others like me for the Kingdom. I answered God's call on my life to be an ordained and licensed servant of the Lord on February 23, 2012.

Today, my passion and reason for living is to let "the least of these" know the true and eternal freedom available by grace alone through faith alone in Jesus Christ alone.

I pray the Holy Spirit continues to work through me to bring the hope, love and grace of Jesus to many who are unloved, lost, hurting, forgotten, needy, despised, depressed and forsaken – people who are even now just like I once was.

I am humbly and eternally grateful for another chance to start over! He is not the God of second chances; rather, He is the God of another chance. His unlimited love, grace and mercy are always available to anyone who comes to Him in humility and sincerity. He gives us an unlimited number of chances.

My feelings are like those of Paul when he wrote to Timothy nearly 2,000 years ago:

> "I thank Christ Jesus our Lord, who has given me strength, that He considered me faithful, appointing me to His service. Even though I was once a blasphemer and a persecutor and a violent man, I was shown mercy because I acted in ignorance and unbelief. The grace of our Lord was poured out on me abundantly, along with the faith and love that are in Christ Jesus. Here is a trustworthy saying that deserves full acceptance: Christ Jesus came into the world to save sinners – of

whom I am the worst. But for that very reason I was shown mercy so that in me, the worst of sinners, Christ Jesus might display His unlimited patience as an example for those who would believe on Him and receive eternal life. Now to the King eternal, immortal, invisible, the only God, be honor and glory for ever and ever. Amen."

(I Timothy 1:12-17)

In sincerity, truth and love I am, and will remain, a humble, grateful child of our Father, and a radical follower of the Lord Jesus Christ, by His Holy Spirit in me!

Stephen

P.S. – Perhaps I should consider changing the title of this testimony to:

"From Park Avenue... to Park Bench...to Prison...to Preacher!"

YOU CAN HAVE "THE REAL THING"

"The Real Thing" has nothing to do with "religion."

Rather, it is an intimate personal relationship with our Heavenly Father, because of the finished work of Jesus at the Cross. The Holy Spirit comes and seals us as His very own, and begins an ongoing work in us to conform us to the image of Christ Jesus.

You can begin this exciting and abundant life today. It will continue throughout all eternity.

First, acknowledge and confess that you have sinned against God.

Second, renounce your sins – determine that you are not going back to them. Turn away from sin. Turn to God.

Third, by faith receive Christ into your heart. Surrender your life completely to Him. He will come to live in your heart by the Holy Spirit.

You can do this right now.

Start by simply talking to God. You can pray a prayer like this:

"Oh God, I am a sinner. I'm sorry for my sin. I want to turn from my sin. Please forgive me. I believe Jesus Christ is Your Son; I believe He died on the Cross for my sin and You raised Him to life. I want to trust Him as my Savior and follow Him as my Lord from this day forward, forevermore. Lord Jesus, I put my trust in You and surrender my life to You. Please come into my life and fill me with your Holy Spirit. In Jesus' Name. Amen."

If you just said this prayer, and you meant it with all your heart, we believe you just got Saved and are now Born Again in Christ Jesus as a totally new person.

"Therefore, if anyone is in Christ, he is a new creation; the old has gone, the new has come!" (II Corinthians 5:17)

We urge you to go "all in and all out for the All in All"! (Pastor Mark Batterson, <u>All In</u>)

We suggest you follow the Lord in water baptism at your earliest opportunity. Water baptism is an outward symbol of the inward change that follows your salvation and re-birth.

The grace of God Himself gives you the desire and ability to surrender completely to the Holy Spirit's work in and through you (Philippians 2:13).

The Baptism in the Holy Spirit is His empowerment for you.

YOU CAN RECEIVE THE BAPTISM IN THE HOLY SPIRIT

The Baptism in the Holy Spirit is a separate experience and a Holy privilege granted to those who ask. This is God's own power to enable you to live an abundant, overcoming life. The Bible says it is the same power that raised Jesus from the dead (Romans 1:4; 8:11; II Cor. 4:13-14; 1 Peter 3:18).

Have you asked the Father for Jesus to baptize you (immerse you) in the Holy Spirit (Luke 3:16)? If you ask the Father, He will give Him to you (Luke 11:13). Have you allowed the "rivers of living water" to flow from within you (John 7:38-39)? Our Father desires for us to walk in all His fullness by His Holy Spirit.

The power to witness, and live your life the way Jesus did in intimate relationship with the Father, comes from asking Jesus to baptize you in the Holy Spirit. To receive this baptism, pray along these lines:

Abba Father and my Lord Jesus,

Thank you for giving me your Spirit to live inside me. I am saved by grace through faith in Jesus. I ask you now to baptize me in the Holy Ghost with Your fire and power. I fully receive it through faith just like I did my salvation. Now, Holy Spirit, come and rise up within me as I praise God! Fill me up Jesus! I fully expect to receive my prayer language as You give me utterance. In Jesus' Name. Amen.

Now, out loud, begin to praise and glorify JESUS, because He is the baptizer of the Holy Spirit! From deep in your spirit, tell Him, "I love you, I thank you, I praise you, Jesus."

Repeat this as you feel joy and gratefulness bubble up from deep inside you. Speak those words and syllables you receive – not in your own language, but the heavenly language given to you by the Holy Spirit. Allow this joy to come out of you in syllables of a language your own mind does not already know. That will be your prayer language the Spirit will use through you when you don't know how to pray (Romans 8:26-28). It is not the "gift of tongues" for public use, therefore it does not require a public interpretation.

You have to surrender and use your own vocal chords to verbally express your new prayer language. The Holy Spirit is a gentleman. He will not force you to speak. Don't be concerned with how it sounds. It is a heavenly language!

Worship Him! Praise Him! Use your heavenly language by praying in the Spirit every day! Paul urges us to "pray in the Spirit on all occasions with all kinds of prayers and requests." (Ephesians 6:18)

CONTACT US

We would love to hear your feedback or answer your questions.

- We would especially like to know if you made a decision to receive Jesus into your heart and prayed the prayer of Salvation on page 41. Or maybe you had prayed a similar prayer before, but this is the first time you really meant it from your heart. Tell us about your decision.

- Perhaps you made a decision to rededicate your life to Christ – to go "all in and all out" for Jesus! If so, we would like to know so we can encourage you. Please write to us.

- If you prayed the prayer to ask Jesus to baptize you in the Holy Spirit, please tell us. When you do, we will send you more material on the Holy Spirit.

As a further aid and encouragement, we would like to teach you more about how to follow Jesus – how to be a true disciple. A disciple is a "disciplined learner" and we want to share many truths with you about how to have an intimate relationship with God the Father, by the Holy Spirit. Jesus came to reconcile us to the Father. We want to help you develop a meaningful relationship with Him.

Please ask for us to include you in our Discipleship Program whereby you will receive an encouraging teaching every two months or so. This is not the kind of lesson you are required to fill in and send back to us. You must only desire to be encouraged regularly in the Lord, and be willing to prayerfully study the materials. That's all.

Please send your comments, questions and feedback to:

Freedom in Jesus Prison Ministries
Attn: Stephen - JHR
P.O. Box 939
Levelland, TX 79336

Don't forget to ask us to put you on our discipleship mailing list.

If you or your loved ones want to know more about
our ministry, our website is www.fijm.org

We pray you are blessed abundantly by our Father as you seek Him daily with all your heart, forever abiding IN Christ Jesus by His Holy Spirit in you!

I PRAISE HIM!

In the middle of despair, I lost all hope

Prayer was a foreign language I could not
understand nor comprehend

Redemption hid itself from my understanding

Addictions dominated my past and determined my future

Inside me a black hole sucked up all light, love and faith

Suicidal thoughts, means and devices disabled
my days and stole my nights

Endless cycles of guilt, shame, regret, inadequacy
and depression imprisoned me

Heaven intervened through God's grace, love and mercy

I finally realized I must forgive myself to accept forgiveness from Him

My remaining days will be a testimony to the life,
hope and salvation found in Christ

I praise Him!

Stephen Canup

I CHALLENGE YOU!!

God is able to transform your life in the same way He did mine.

But you must understand that He rewards those who diligently and earnestly seek Him (**Hebrews 11:6**); and, that you are transformed by renewing your mind through applying the principles in His Word to your daily life (**Romans 12:1-2**).

I challenge you to:

- **Re-read** this book often. When you do, ask the Holy Spirit to help you apply His Truth to your life.

- **Look up** every scripture reference in this book. Mark the verses in your own Bible. Memorize the ones that mean the most to you.

- **Study** the scriptural principles in this book in small groups. Sharing concepts from the Word with others helps you learn and apply them to your life.

- **Share** your own testimony with others. You "overcome" when you personally testify to yourself and others what the Blood of Jesus has done in your own life (see **Revelation 12:11**).

- **Loan** this book to at least three others if your facility permits you to do so. As an ambassador for Christ (see II **Corinthians 5:18-20**), please use this book as a tool to reach the lost. After sharing it with them, tell them then to write to me and request their own copy of the book so they can study it and loan it to others. Each person who wants one must write me individually because I can only send one book to each person.

- **Pray** daily for me and for our ministry. We need your prayers. At your first opportunity, begin a program of regular giving to us so we can better minister to others and provide them free books like we have done for you.

As you do these things, I pray God the Father blesses you and your family abundantly in every way, every day, IN Christ Jesus, through His Holy Spirit working powerfully in and through you!

INFORMATION FOR
FURTHER STUDY
AND APPLICATION

PRAYERS OF SUBMISSION

Daily Prayer of Surrender and Submission

Father God, I humbly surrender and submit myself fully to You and your leadership by Your Holy Spirit.

Lord, please forgive me for both my willful and my unintentional sins. Help me to freely and fully forgive others as You forgive me.

Father, I submit willingly and completely to your Hand as The Potter. Re-make me into the person You want me to be for the plan You have for me in Your perfect will. As You do, conform me to the image of Jesus by the sanctifying work of Your Holy Spirit.

Father, by Your grace help me to always be a grateful, humble heir of all Your promises; an obedient, faithful servant of all Your commands; a persistent, bold witness of Your salvation through Jesus; and, a loving, trusting child full of Your love. I surrender to Your Holy Spirit's leadership.

Let me be patient and persevering in prayer, ever watchful and responsive for opportunities to bless others as You have blessed me. Empower me Father with Your grace, through the Spirit of Jesus in me, to diligently seek You and Your eternal Kingdom, so that I will not be distracted and overcome with the temptations and temporary pleasures of this alien world. In everything I think, say and do today, Father, let me continually glorify and honor You.

I love You, Jesus. I praise You and adore You for first loving me. Thank You for being made sin for me so that I am made righteous in You. Please love and bless others through me today as I seek to know and do Your perfect will for my life. I want to be led today by Your Holy Spirit in me.

In the power of the blood of Jesus, and the authority of His Name I pray. Amen.

Prayer of Submissive Obedience in a Particular Area

Father, You are worthy of all praise, honor, and glory. I adore You. I worship You. I praise Your Holy Name.

Lord, You have been so patient with me, and I thank You. I also recognize Your still, small voice, speaking to me about an area of my life that needs resolution. You have been reminding me of my need to move ahead in this certain area, and I confess that I have not yet obeyed You. Please forgive me for my hesitation.

Today, I declare that I will take the step of faith You have spoken to me about. Lord, in regard to this step that I have been hesitant to take, I put away all my reluctance now, and I pledge to You that I will obey You.

And Lord, in those matters where I have been doing what You would prefer that I not do, I lay them aside, so that I can make room to do what You want me to do.

This is the way I choose to walk with you from now on. Laying aside my hesitancy and stubbornness, I step boldly, choosing You and Your purposes for my life. I declare that I will follow You in obedience.

Thank You, Lord! In Jesus' Name I pray. Amen.

BAPTISM IN THE HOLY SPIRIT
SCRIPTURAL BASIS AND AUTHORITY

John the Baptist taught about the Holy Spirit:
Matthew 3:11 "I baptize you with water for repentance. But after me will come one who is more powerful than I, whose sandals I am not fit to carry. He will baptize you with the Holy Spirit and with fire."

Jesus Christ had to have the Holy Spirit:
Matthew 3:16-17 As soon as Jesus was baptized, he went up out of the water. At that moment heaven was opened, and he saw the Spirit of God descending like a dove and lighting on him. And a voice from heaven said, "This is my Son, whom I love; with him I am well pleased."

Jesus Needed to be Led by the Holy Spirit:
Matthew 4:1 Then Jesus was led by the Spirit into the desert to be tempted by the devil.

Luke 4:1 Jesus, full of the Holy Spirit, returned from the Jordan and was led by the Spirit in the desert...

Jesus was Empowered by the Holy Spirit:
Luke 4:14 Jesus returned to Galilee in the power of the Spirit, and news about him spread through the whole countryside.

Luke 4:18-19 "The Spirit of the Lord is on me, because he has anointed me to preach good news to the poor. He has sent me to proclaim freedom for the prisoners and recovery of sight for the blind, to release the oppressed, to proclaim the year of the Lord's favor."

Acts 10:38 ...how God anointed Jesus of Nazareth with the Holy Spirit and power, and how he went around doing good and healing all who were under the power of the devil, because God was with him.

YOU can Have the Holy Spirit as a GIFT:

Luke 11:11-13 "Which of you fathers, if your son asks for a fish, will give him a snake instead? Or if he asks for an egg, will give him a scorpion? If you then, though you are evil, know how to give good gifts to your children, how much more will your Father in heaven give the Holy Spirit to those who ask him!"

John 7:37-39 On the last and greatest day of the Feast, Jesus stood and said in a loud voice, "If anyone is thirsty, let him come to me and drink. Whoever believes in me, as the Scripture has said, streams of living water will flow from within him." By this he meant the Spirit, whom those who believed in him were later to receive. Up to that time the Spirit had not been given, since Jesus had not yet been glorified.

Revelation 22:17 The Spirit and the bride say, "Come!" And let him who hears say, "Come!" Whoever is thirsty, let him come; and whoever wishes, let him take the free gift of the water of life.

John 14:16-17 "And I will ask the Father, and he will give you another Counselor to be with you forever-- the Spirit of truth. The world cannot accept him, because it neither sees him nor knows him. But you know him, for he lives with you and will be in you."

Acts 1:4-5 On one occasion, while he was eating with them, he gave them this command: "Do not leave Jerusalem, but wait for the gift my Father promised, which you have heard me speak about. For John baptized with water, but in a few days you will be baptized with the Holy Spirit."

Acts 2:1-4 When the day of Pentecost came, they were all together in one place. Suddenly a sound like the blowing of a violent wind came from heaven and filled the whole house where they were sitting. They saw what seemed to be tongues of fire that separated and came to rest on each of them. All of them were filled with the Holy Spirit and began to speak in other tongues as the Spirit enabled them.

The Baptism of the Holy Spirit is Separate from Water Baptism:

John 20:21-22 Again Jesus said, "Peace be with you! As the Father has sent me, I am sending you." And with that he breathed on them and said, "Receive the Holy Spirit."

Acts 8:14-17 When the apostles in Jerusalem heard that Samaria had accepted the word of God, they sent Peter and John to them. When they arrived, they prayed for them that they might receive the Holy Spirit, because the Holy Spirit had not yet come upon any of them; they had simply been baptized into the name of the Lord Jesus. Then Peter and John placed their hands on them, and they received the Holy Spirit.

Acts 19:1-6 While Apollos was at Corinth, Paul took the road through the interior and arrived at Ephesus. There he found some disciples and asked them, "Did you receive the Holy Spirit when you believed?" They answered, "No, we have not even heard that there is a Holy Spirit." So Paul asked, "Then what baptism did you receive?" "John's baptism," they replied. Paul said, "John's baptism was a baptism of repentance. He told the people to believe in the one coming after him, that is, in Jesus." On hearing this, they were baptized into the name of the Lord Jesus. When Paul placed his hands on them, the Holy Spirit came on them, and they spoke in tongues and prophesied.

THE HOLY SPIRIT

The Holy Spirit is the third person in the Trinity. He is fully God. He is eternal, omniscient, omnipresent, has a will, and can speak. He is alive. He is a person. He is not as visible in the Bible as the Son or Father because His ministry is to bear witness of them (John 15:26). However, as you begin to focus on Him, you will see how very important He is to us!

In the Old Testament the Hebrew word ruwach (pronounced roo'-akh) was used when talking about the Spirit. This word literally means WIND or BREATH. In the New Testament the Greek word pneuma (pronounced pnyoo'-mah) was used which means the BREATH or a BREEZE. We can literally think of the Holy Spirit as the "BREATH OF GOD."

Throughout the ages, many people have thought of the Holy Spirit as more of a "thing", or a "force", than a "Person." Nothing could be further from the truth. In fact, as we begin to know the Person of the Holy Spirit, we will want to have a closer relationship with Him just as we would the Father or Son.

Although the word Trinity is not mentioned in the Bible, we know God is three in one. There are three very distinct Persons that make up the Godhead. They are all equal in every way. The Holy Spirit is a Person the same as the Father and the Son are Persons within the Trinity. There are some who believe the Holy Spirit is merely a force. If this were true, then He could not speak (Acts 13:2); He could not be grieved (Eph. 4:30); and He would not have a will (I Cor. 12:11).

The truth is that the Holy Spirit is a Person the same as the Father and the Son are Persons within the Trinity.

By careful study of the following scriptures about the Person of God the Holy Spirit, you will be able to better understand His Presence and Power living in you:

HIS NAMES	HIS ATTRIBUTES	SYMBOLS OF	SINS AGAINST	POWER IN CHRIST'S LIFE
God *Acts 5:3-4*	Eternal *Heb. 9:14*	Dove *Matt. 3:16*	Blasphemy *Matt. 12:31*	Conceived of *Matt. 1:18,20*
Lord *2 Cor. 3:18*	Omnipotent *Luke 1:35*	Wind *Acts 2:1-4*	Resist (Unbelief) *Acts 7:51*	Baptism *Matt. 3:16*
Spirit *1 Cor. 2:10*	Omnipresent *Psalm 139:7-10*	Fire *Acts 2:3*	Insult *Heb. 10:29*	Led by *Luke 4:1*
Spirit of God *1 Cor. 3:16*	Will *1 Cor. 12:11*	Living Waters *John 7:38-39* *1 Cor. 12:13*	Lied to *Acts 5:3*	Filled with Power *Luke 4:14,18*
Spirit of Truth *John 15:26*	Loves *Rom. 15:30*	.....	Grieved *Eph. 4:30*	Witness of Jesus *John 15:26*
Eternal Spirit *Heb. 9:14*	Speaks *Acts 8:29; 13:2*	.....	Quench *1 Thess. 5:19*	Raised Jesus *Rom. 8:11*
The Person of God the Holy Spirit				

It is important to understand the Holy Spirit is truly God because of the fact that if we are born again He lives in us. What we allow ourselves to become a part of we are inviting God to be part of. I Cor. 6:19.

Four important principles to remember:

1. The Holy Spirit is God. Like the Father and the Son, He is a Person, not a "force", a "thing", or an "it".

2. We cannot focus on the Holy Spirit too much. Why? What is the Holy Spirit's mission? To reveal Jesus. What is Jesus' mission? To reveal the Father. What about the Father.....to send Jesus and the Holy Spirit so we can come to Him. Perfect Harmony. They never had a crisis management meeting in Heaven. They never tried to sit down and work things out. They never had a power struggle amongst themselves.

58

3. The Holy Spirit gives gifts for use in ministry and empowers effective ministry. I Cor. 12:7-11

4. The Holy Spirit gives us fruit which develops in us Christ-like character. Gal. 5:22-23

Qualities that a person has.... (A "force" or "thing" does not):
1. The Holy Spirit has intellect. I Cor. 2:10

2. The Holy Spirit has knowledge. I Cor. 2:11

3. The Holy Spirit has emotions. Ephesians 4:30

4. The Holy Spirit has his own will and he makes decisions. Acts 16:6

5. The Holy Spirit loves. Romans 15:30

Things only a person would do (a "force" or "thing" does not):
1. He teaches you things about God and yourself. John 14:26

2. He tells the truth. John 15:26

3. He guides. John 16:13

4. He convinces. John 16:8

5. He prays for you. Romans 8:26-27

6. He commands. Acts 13:2

The Holy Spirit was on the scene long before the day of Pentecost:
- He moved upon the face of the waters and was the active agent in creation. Jesus was the Word, the Holy Spirit moved. John 1:1,14; Genesis 1:2

- The Holy Spirit gave us the Word of God. 2 Peter 1:20-21

- The Holy Spirit regenerates our spirit when we accept Jesus Christ into our life. John 3:6

In fact, the Holy Spirit has always worked hand-in-hand with Jesus Christ:
- His birth. Matthew 1:20

- The life and ministry of Jesus. Luke 4:1; Luke 4:18

- His death and offering Himself as the perfect sacrifice. Hebrews 9:14

- The resurrection of Jesus – Actually all 3 members of the Godhead had a part in the resurrection! FATHER (Eph. 1:19-20); SON (John 10:18); HOLY SPIRIT (Romans 1:4).

The main purpose of the Holy Spirit is to tell us about Jesus and Glorify Him. John 16:13-14

Pentecost:
- Jesus said it was imperative that He go or the Spirit would not be sent. John 16:7
- Jesus felt it important enough for them to wait until the Spirit came to empower them. Acts 1:4-8
- Jesus' own mother needed the baptism of the Holy Spirit to be an effective witness. Acts 1:14
- On the day of Pentecost, the believers who were assembled in the Upper Room experienced a new Baptism, the one which John referred to. Acts 2:1-4

MINISTRY OF THE BAPTISM
OF THE HOLY SPIRIT

Hebrews 6:17 Malachi 3:6	God's purpose is unchanging, confirmed and guaranteed.
Matthew 28:20	He is always with us through His Holy Spirit.
John 14:12 Matthew 28:18	The Holy Spirit enables us to do greater works than Jesus through the authority of Jesus given to us.
Hebrews 13:8	"Jesus Christ is same yesterday, today, and forever."

Who is the Holy Spirit?

Genesis 1:2,26	The Holy Spirit is the 3rd person of the Trinity.
1 Corinthians 12:11	He has a will.
Ephesians 4:30	He has feelings.
Luke 1:35	He conceived Jesus.

The Holy Spirit's Ministry

John 14:15-18 John 15:26-27 John 16:13-15	The Holy Spirit has been given to us that we may let Jesus work in and through us (our sole purpose in life is to carry the Holy Spirit in our body and let Him work through us that the Father might be glorified in the Son).
Romans 8:26-27	He makes intercession for us when we don't know how to pray.
John 14:16	He is our Helper and Teacher.
John 16:8	The Holy Spirit convicts. It is not our place to judge others; we are to let the Holy Spirit convict them.
Ephesians 4:30	He seals us for the day of redemption.
1 Corinthians 12:7-11	He distributes His manifestation gifts to us.

Hebrews 10:15	He witnesses to us (bears witness).
Romans 8:11	The Holy Spirit dwells in us and gives life to our mortal bodies
Acts 9:31	He comforts and encourages us.
Galatians 5:22-23	He bears fruit in us.
John 16:14	The Holy Spirit always glorifies Jesus.
1 Corinthians 12:13 and Acts 1:5	He baptizes.
Acts 1:8 and Luke 24:49	He endues power.

Five Accounts in the book of Acts of the Baptism of the Holy Spirit

Acts 2:4, Acts 8:14-25, Acts 9:17-20,
Acts 10:44-48, Acts 19:1-7

How to Receive the Baptism of the Holy Spirit
Jesus is the Baptizer of the Holy Spirit: Matthew 3:11, Mark 1:8, Luke 3:16

Believe, Pray, Ask, Receive

MORE INFORMATION ON THE BAPTISM IN THE HOLY SPIRIT

Scripture References

The Day of Pentecost	Acts 2
Spirit of power, love and a sound mind	2 Timothy 1:7
Sending another Counselor	John 14:15-20; John 16:7
Quenching the Spirit	1 Thessalonians 5:19-22
Receive the Holy Spirit	John 20:22
Joel's Prophecy	Joel 2:28-32
Test the Spirits	1 Thessalonians 5:21; 1 John 4:1
You will know them by their fruit	Matthew 7:15-20

Some Holy Spirit Manifestations in Scripture

- There is no comprehensive list... the Bible does not record all possible experiences (John 21:25).

- Falling under the influence of the Spirit (Revelation 1:17; Matthew 17:6; John 18:6; Acts 9:4-8; Ezekiel 1:28; 3:23, 43:3, 44:4; Daniel 8:17-18; Daniel 10:8-9).

- Drunk in the Spirit (Acts 2:15; Ephesians 5:18).

- Laughter and joy (Romans 14:17; Galatians 5:22; Psalm 126:2-3; Genesis 21:3,6; 1 Peter 1:8).

- Trembling and terror (Daniel 8:17-18, 10:7-11; Matthew 17:6; Matthew 28:4).

- Shaking (Exodus 19:16-18; Acts 4:31; Isaiah 6:4).

- Speechless (Daniel 10:15-19; Ezekiel 3:26; Luke 1:22).

- Weeping (2 Chronicles 34:27; Hosea 12:4; Matthew 26:75; Luke 19:41; 2 Corinthians 7:10; Revelation 5:4; Hebrews 5:7).

- Trances (Acts 10:10, 22:17; Numbers 24:3-4).

- Pockets of power (1 Samuel 19:19-24).

- Traveling by the Spirit (Acts 8:39-40; Ezekiel 3:14, 8:3, 11:24; 2 Corinthians 12:1-4, Revelation 4:1-2).

- Fire (Exodus 3:2, 24:17, 40:38; Leviticus 9:24; Luke 3:16; Acts 2:3; 1 Thessalonians 5:19; Hebrews 12:29).

CONFESSIONS FOR EVERY DAY

Loved One in Christ - Build your faith and claim God's promises for yourself by reading these confessions of God's Word aloud (thoughtfully and prayerfully – with conviction) every day. Keep doing it until they are your thoughts so that you can use the Word against Satan to "take every thought captive" when he attacks your mind! To "confess" is to say the same thing as God, so that as the Word transforms your mind, His thoughts become your thoughts! Confess these daily at least once – early morning is best so you are "armed and dangerous" when Satan attacks during the day! Before bedtime is good too so you are protected as you rest.

- I am not just an ordinary man/woman.
  I'm a child of the living God.

- I am not just a person; I'm an heir of God, and a joint heir with Jesus Christ. I'm not "just an old sinner", I am a new creation in Jesus, my Lord. I'm part of a chosen generation, a Royal Priesthood, a Holy Nation. I'm one of God's people. I am His. I am a living witness of His grace, mercy and love!

- I have been crucified with Christ and I no longer live, but Christ lives in me! The life I live in the body, I live by the faith of the Son of God, who loved me, and gave Himself for me. When the devil tries to resurrect the "old man", I will rebuke him and remind him sternly that I am aware of his tricks, lures, lies and deception. The "old man" is dead. My "new man" knows all old things are passed away - all things have become new!

- I'm not under guilt or condemnation. I refuse discouragement, for it is not of God. God is the God of all encouragement. There is therefore now no condemnation for those in Christ Jesus. Satan is a liar. I will not listen to his accusations.

- I gird up my loins of my mind. I am cleansed in the Blood. No weapon formed against me shall prosper, and I shall condemn every tongue rising against me in judgment. I am accepted in the beloved. If God be for me, who can be against me?

- My mind is being renewed by the Word of God. I pull down strongholds; I cast down imaginations; I bring every thought captive to the obedience of Christ.

- As the Father loves Jesus, so Jesus loves me. I'm the righteousness of God in Christ. I'm not slave of sin; I am a slave of God and a slave of righteousness. I continue in His Word; I know the truth and I practice it, so the truth sets me free.

- Because the Son sets me free, I am free indeed. He who is born of God keeps me, therefore the evil one does not touch me. I've been delivered out of the kingdom of darkness. I am now part of the Kingdom of Light, the Kingdom of God. I don't serve sin any longer. Sin has no dominion over me.

- I will not believe the enemy's lies. He will not intimidate me. He is a liar and the father of lies. Satan is defeated. For this purpose, the Son of God came into this world – to destroy the works of the devil. No longer will he oppress me. Surely, oppression makes a wise person mad. I will get mad at the devil. I defeat him by the Blood of the Lamb, by the word of my testimony as to what He has done for me, not loving my life, even to death.

- I will submit to God. I will resist the devil and he will flee. No temptation will overtake me that is not common to man. God is Faithful and True; He will not let me be tempted beyond my strength, but with the temptation He will also provide the way of escape (Jesus) that I may be able to endure.

- I will stand fast in the liberty with which Christ has made me free. Where the Spirit of the Lord is, there is liberty – not liberty to do what I "want", but freedom to do as I "ought". The law of the Spirit of Life in Christ

Jesus has set me free from the law of sin and death.

- Nothing can separate me from the love of God that is in Christ Jesus, my Lord. His Holy Spirit is my guide, comforter, teacher and best friend! Jesus is my Protector, my Deliverer, my Rewarder, my Refuge, my Strong Tower, my Shepherd, my Light, my Life, my Counselor, my Rock, my Freedom! He is everything to me!

- Christ causes me to triumph. I will reign as a king in life through Christ Jesus. As a young man/woman I am strong. The Word of God abides in me, and I have overcome the evil one. I am more than a conqueror through Christ who loves me. I am an overcomer. I am invincible. I can do all things through Christ who strengthens me. Thanks be to God who gives me the victory through Jesus Christ, my Lord!

Wisdom and Guidance Confessions
- The Spirit of Truth abides in me and teaches me all things, and He guides me into all truths. Therefore, I confess I have perfect knowledge of every situation and circumstance I come up against, for I have the wisdom of God. (John 16:13; James 1:5)

- I trust in the Lord with all my heart and I do not lean or rely on my own understanding. In all my ways I acknowledge Him, and He directs my path. (Proverbs 3:5-6)

- The Lord will perfect that which concerns me, and fulfill His purpose for me. (Psalm 138:8)

- I let the Word of Christ dwell in me richly in all wisdom. (Colossians 3:16)

- I do follow the Good Shepherd, and I know His voice. The voice of a stranger I will not follow. (John 10:4-5)

- Jesus is made unto me wisdom, righteousness, sanctification, and redemption. Therefore, I confess I have the wisdom of God, and I am the righteousness of God in Christ Jesus. (I Cor. 1:30; II Cor. 5:21)

- I am filled with the knowledge of the Lord's will in all wisdom and spiritual understanding. (Colossians 1:9)

- I am a new creation in Christ. I am His workmanship created in Christ Jesus. Therefore, I have the mind of Christ and the wisdom of God is formed within me. (II Cor. 5:17; Ephesians 2:10; I Cor. 2:16)

- I receive the Spirit of wisdom and revelation in the knowledge of Him, the eyes of my understanding being enlightened. I am not conformed to this world but I am transformed by the renewing of my mind. My mind is renewed by the Word of God. (Ephesians 1:17-18; Romans 12:2)

I AM...
- I am forgiven. (Col. 1:13-14)
- I am saved by grace through faith. (Eph. 2:8)
- I am delivered from the powers of darkness. (Col. 1:13)
- I am led by the Spirit of God. (Rom. 8:14)
- I am kept in safety wherever I go. (Psalm 91:11-12)
- I am getting all my needs met by Jesus. (Phil. 4:19)
- I am casting all my cares on Jesus. (I Peter 5:7)
- I am not anxious or worried about anything. (Phil. 4:6)
- I am strong in the Lord and in the power of His might. (Eph. 6:10)
- I am doing all things through Christ who strengthens me. (Phil. 4:13)
- I am observing and doing the Lord's commandments. (Deut. 28:13)

- I am blessed going in and blessed going out. (Deut. 28:6)
- I am above only and not beneath. (Deut. 28:13)
- I am blessed with all spiritual blessings. (Eph. 1:3)
- I am healed by His stripes. (I Peter 2:24)
- I am more than a conqueror. (Romans 8:37)
- I am an overcomer by the Blood of the Lamb and the word of my testimony. (Rev. 12:11)
- I am not moved by what I see. (II Cor. 4:8-9)
- I am walking by faith and not by sight. (II Cor. 5:7)
- I am daily overcoming the Devil. (I John 4:4)
- I am casting down vain imaginations. (II Cor. 10:4)
- I am bringing every thought into captivity. (II Cor.10:5)
- I am not conformed to this world, but I am being transformed by renewing my mind. (Romans 12:1-2)
- I am blessing the Lord at all times and continually praising the Lord with my mouth. (Psalm 34:1)
- I am a child of God. (Romans 8:16)

PERSONALIZED DAILY PRAYERS

Loved one in Christ: These passages of scripture from Paul, David, and Isaiah have been personalized for you. They are powerful prayers, by powerful men, to the Most Powerful! As you pray God's Word back to Him, He is pleased, for He has told us to put Him in remembrance of His Word. Do you think He needs to be reminded? Like He forgot? No, we are the ones who need to be reminded. We claim these awesome promises for ourselves. Pray these daily as the Spirit leads you. You will be richly blessed in doing so.

In the name of Jesus,

I praise you Lord from my soul. From my inmost being I praise your Holy name. I praise you Lord from my soul. I will not forget all your benefits – you forgive all my sins and heal all my diseases. You redeemed my life from the pit and crowned me with your love and compassion. You satisfy my desires with good things so that my youth is renewed like an eagle's. Amen. (Psalm 103:1-5)

In the name of Jesus,

As I dwell in the shelter of the Most High I will rest in the shadow of the Almighty. I will say of you Lord, "You are my refuge and my fortress. You are my God and I will trust in you." Surely you will save me from the fowler's snare and from the deadly pestilence. You will cover me with your feathers, and under your wings I will find refuge; your faithfulness will be my shield and rampart.

I will not fear the terror of night nor the arrow that flies by day, nor the pestilence that stalks in the darkness, nor the plague that destroys at midday. A thousand may fall at my side, ten thousand by my right hand, but it will not come near me.

I will observe with my eyes and see the punishment of the wicked. I will make the Most High my dwelling – the Lord is my refuge – so that no harm will befall me, no disaster will come near my tent. God, you will command your angels concerning me to guard me in all my ways; they will lift me up in their hands, so that I will not strike my foot against a stone. I will tread upon the lion and the cobra; I will trample the great lion and the serpent.

Lord, you said because I love you, you will rescue me. You will protect me, for I acknowledge your name. I will call upon you and you will answer me; you will be with me in trouble, you will deliver me and honor me. With long life will you satisfy me and show me your salvation. Amen. (Psalm 91)

In the name of Jesus,
No weapon forged against me will prevail and I will refute every tongue that accuses me. This is my heritage as a servant of the Lord, and this is my vindication from you. Amen. (Isaiah 54:17)

In the name of Jesus,
I keep asking that you, God of my Lord Jesus Christ, my glorious Father, may give me the Spirit of wisdom and revelation that I may know you better. I pray also that the eyes of my heart may be enlightened in order that I may know the hope to which you have called me, the riches of your glorious inheritance in the saints, and your incomparably great power for us who believe. That power is like the working of your mighty strength, which you exerted in Christ when you raised Him from the dead and seated Him at your right hand in heavenly realms, far above all rule and authority, power and dominion, and every title that can be given, not only in the present age but also in the one to come. And you, God, placed all things under His feet and appointed Him to be over everything for the church, which is His body, the fullness of Him who fills everything in every way. Amen. (Ephesians 1:17-23)

In the name of Jesus,
I pray that out of your glorious riches you may strengthen me with power through your Spirit in my inner being, so that Christ may dwell in my heart through faith. And I pray that as I am rooted and established in love, I may have power, together with all the saints, to grasp how wide and long and high and deep is the love of Christ, and that I may know this love that surpasses knowledge – that I may be filled to the measure of all your fullness.

Now to you, God, who is able to do immeasurably more than all I ask or imagine, according to your power that is at work within me, to you be glory in the church and in Christ Jesus throughout all generations, forever and ever! Amen. (Ephesians 3:16-21)

In the name of Jesus,

This also is my prayer: that my love may abound more and more in knowledge and depth of insight, so that I may be able to discern what is best and may be pure and blameless until the day of Christ, filled with the fruit of righteousness that comes through Jesus Christ – to the glory and praise of you, God. Amen. (Philippians 1:9-11)

In the name of Jesus,

I pray that you fill me with the knowledge of your will through all spiritual wisdom and understanding. I pray this in order that I may live a life worthy of the Lord Jesus and please Him in every way: bearing fruit in every good work, growing in the knowledge of you, God, so that I may be strengthened with all power according to your glorious might so that I may have great endurance and patience and joyfully give you thanks. Amen. (Colossians 1:9b-11)